Ideas For Prison Wardens

Leadership Is Not Easy

Reverend Mike Wanner

Table Of Contents

Introduction

I have been writing a lot about prisons and realized that the most difficult position in the whole instituition may be yours. Here is the list of books that I have written recently:

1. *Angel Raphael Speaks Volume 4: Angels, Addicts, Alcoholics & Prisoners – Oh Yeah!*
2. *Angel Raphael Speaks Volume 5:* Prisoners Caring for Alcoholics - Australia In Miniature Projects Intro
3. *Angel Raphael Speaks Volume 6:* Prisoners Caring for Addicts - Australia In Miniature For Addicts
4. *Prison Jobs Now: Providing Care For Addicts And   Alcoholics*
5. *Angel Raphael Speaks - Prisons* (A Kindle only book -2013)
6. *Contained Care Communities Concept*
7. *Australia In Miniature*
8. *Prison Possibilities Dial   ogue Series: Concept*
9. *Prison Possibilities Dialogue Series: Volume 2 Dialogues*
10. *Prison Possibilities Dialogue Series: Volume 3 Dialogues*
11. *Prison Possibilities Dialogue Series: Volume 4 Dialogues*
12. *Prison Possibilities Dialogue Series: Volume 5 Dialogues*
13. *Prison Possibilities Voluntary Exile: Concept*
14. *Prison Possibilities Correction Coaches: Concept*
15. *Prison Possibilities for Mexicans: Is A Boat Better than A Wall?*
16. *Prison Possibilities Family Time:* A Reason to Thrive!
17. Prison Genius Pool: *"So Much Genius In Jail"*
18. *Prison Possibilities Access Systems: Prisoner Access by Request*
19. *Prisoner's Lawyers Can Save The American Economy: Make A Buck Doing It & Be Thanked!*
20. *Prisoner Family Talks, Days, Stays & Vacations: Connecting Helps Healing*
21. *Prisoner Writing Projects: Write To Heal, Start Over & Reconnect*
22. *Prison Cell Clearing & Blessing: Clear Entities, Chase Ghosts, and & Create Sacred Space*
23. *Prisoner Professors*
24. *Prison Reiki? Maybe Someday? A Gateway To Help Heal Prisons & America?*
25. *Judges and An Angel Rule On Possibilities:We Can Cut Sentences & Prison Costs*

1 - Why I am Writing This Book

I have been absolutely amazed at the complexity of the whole prison situation and the variety of rules and authorities that oversee the various facilities. The position that you are in has to be among the most stressful of all time.

I want to offer some ideas here for your consideration. My ideas will probably not be boring but they may be impractical in your particular facility.

Please do not consider this book as derogatory because my intention is the direct opposite. I am not involved in the prison dynamics which take most of your days so I am trying to offer some objectivity.

If nothing here is helpful then please accept my apologies. If anything helps I would like to know what.

If you have any areas that you can discuss privately but not publicly, I would be happy to hear from you about that. If there is any topic that you would like to invite feedback about, I encourage your inquiry.

I may not have anything to offer but I have always found value in opinions from people who casually observe situations without being involved in the drama. Objectivity can offer perspectives from observations that cannot normally be seen by those with a patterned experience and further consideration can extract ideas that are fresh and unconditional.

2 - Areas That Seem To Need Attention

Prisons can be rather large and impersonal and that may lead to some attitudes that further complicate the lives of those who live or work in incarceration facilities.

In America, freedom is treasured and independence is the predominate motivator for creativity. In prison, control seems to be important to maintain order.

In this book, I would like to toss out some alternative thoughts that may seem to allow less rigidity but may actually offer possibilities of more freedom for all without a struggle.

So let's Talk about:

Congestion
Monitoring and Supervision
Independence
Competencies
Segmentation
Message Marketing
Feelings
Coaching
Mental Health
Addictions
Jobs
Wrap Up From Volume 4
An Addictions Success Story

3 - Congestion

As I read about the interchanges between prisoners and corrections officer, I am always struck by references that seem to make situations too close for comfort. The number of corrections officers per prisoner can vary widely by facility.

Different types of facilities carry intrinsic process variations as set by the goals of the facility. Most facilities seem to be built on technology and design which is from a different era.

Of course, the ideal is to have sleek new facilities but realistically the wish lists have to be tamed by practical cost and budget settings. The latest and greatest may not always be available.

Modern does contribute to the the spirit and function of a facility and it can influence levels of personal peace for both prisoners and corrections officers. A principle that can avoid congestion and system stress is called fluidity.

Control of people and things as they flow through a facility can be controlled by timing so that the flow is smooth and there is minimal need for waiting that could test the patience of people.

Historically flow control systems could be very expensive and complicated but in recent times, cost have become more manageable.

Great value and control could be found in a systematic increase in flow control security checkpoints that automatically keep groups in an optimal control perspective for security and peace.

4 - Monitoring and Supervision

Flow patterns within facilities can be adjusted over time on a continuing basis so that security is maintainable while seemingly given prisoners more options, freedom and peace.

Correction officers likely know the most important places where game playing to challenge the security team can occur. So little bits of access control can be progressively added to reduce risks and tweak efficiency during any kind of group reaction. It may start as early in the day as the first cell opening.

Meal service could be a very effective time to create flow patterns that can easily be unnoticed by residents. When people are hungry and ready to eat, moving them along at a constant pace while eliminating backups can be most effective in adding tranquility to the process.

Staging of service could be equally satisfying for staff and residents. Perhaps there can be time flows as I talked about in my access book that had incremental flow limits so that a holdup in one point would not lead to a backup in line.

When staff know people and know how they respond, there geverneindividuals could meet up with their fiends in a coffee or dessert area that helps to further move along the process.

Trouble could be avoided by structuring in a spreading out pattern also to keep people who do not tolerate each other in patterns that reduce any inclination for reactive behavior that disrupts the communal peace.

5 - Independence

There may be justification early on for engagement of prisoners in new ways when there is some level of increased awareness of independent choice. The options can be maximized when there is cooperation voluntarily given by those who have skills.

Information gathering is easier when people are trying to make a point about something. A way to facilitate that is to invite participation in events that can provide impetus for participation but not be so wide open that there is a need for handling a mass of information that provides no clear base of knowledge.

Little invitations could go a long way to shifting focus from submission to authority to participation in care for the homestead/house/facility. This could be done in many ways but the ones that rush to my awareness are skill sets and group masterminding that promotes awareness.

I have already written about engagement in some of my Dialogue Series possibilities messages and that concept is viewable online under the Prison Possibilities tab on my website http://www.AngelRaphaelSpeaks.Com. The basic concept and the first six dialogues are all visible there by anyone who has web access.

Hopelessness stifles the wanting of goodness, peace and possibilities for reward. Freedom and Independence foster creativity, community, acceptance, courtesy and peace.

Which of those possibilities would help many?

6 - Competencies

Incarceration is a major setback for prisoners that does not go away quickly. It could be damaging to the psyche of some and that can complicate the job of recooperation and rehabilitation.

Mitigation of psychological damage may be possible by refreshing the memory of the prisoners about the skills and certifications that they had achieved in the past. If they are kept aware of who they were and able to become again then they may be able to avoid the spiral downward that can afflict so many who have had their world shaken.

A simple form could allow them to focus on what they accomplished in the past and may help them to prepare for a restart. They could make a concise document like a dialogue discussed above.

Brevity is important because long documents are not as likely to be read. When you know a bit more about some prisoners, it may be possible to cater to some of their interests and needs sometimes.

At the very least, it would be good to have a list of skill sets and social service type information so that you have an idea of how to handle and comfort residents when they are upset. Knowing people's priorities can provide great efficiency in understanding the big picture for each individual and the whole community.

7 - Segmentation

Earlier mentioning of the access book talked a bit about creating communities of control and flows and processes.

Resources within institutions are usually well regulated to keep costs under control and that has great value in serving the taxpayers. Throughout my other books, I always talk about working with the taxpayers in mind and I would like to encourage you to think in those terms and also outside the box to consider and factor in the bigger societal picture.

While doing that, a new awareness of skill sets can bring more value to the residents. There is a lot of time available to prisoners and the question becomes, is it used wisely?

The concept of segmentation may allow movement in many directions at the same time. Over time with progressive and deliberate selection of programs and methodical implementation of specifically authorized and controlled access to areas that allow freedom, opportunity and education.

When you know the prisoners and their interests, it may be quite easy to add definitive programs that provide peace of mind as well as entertainment.

Blending what is wanted with very very subtle messaging of what is in the highest and best good for the larger community can be productive.

A comparable discipline in the real world akin to this control and sharing is called marketing. You may have heard of it.

8 - Message Marketing

The messaging that seems to be prominent from prisons may not be as positive as prison wardens might like. A level of dissatisfaction can be expected because prison is not a voluntary participation agency.

Respect can go a long way to changing the dynamics between people. Old high school bully dynamics may have their place in training spoiled children to be warriors for military service but even the military seem to be super conscious of how much of that is effective and how much might be abusive if not stopped at the precisely optimal time.

Your job is tougher as you are starting out to create art on a canvas that is not spotless and flawless and new and fresh. The messages that you need to deliver need extreme craftsmanship if they are to be productive.

The first component of message creation needs to show willingness to partner for things that can help to provide a foundation for increased good for all participants. Diligently offering possibilities can lead to a lot of failures caused by lack of participation and that should be embraced as experimentation and not personal failure.

An old expression from our friend Anonymous declared clearly that - "If you throw enough mud against the wall, some of it will stick."

The importance of this effort is the trying because only if you try, can you succeed. Trying can be noticed and respected.

9 - Feelings

It seems evident that the reality of prison is a major issue for many prisoners but there does not seem to be a willingness to confront things. It is not just prisoners who have issues of feelings and taking control of them.

There is a great need in our society to deal with the underlaying emotional turmoil that creates a fertile field from which emotional struggle and societal conflicts surface. I invite you to offer programs that go deeper than prison and seek to understand pre-prison dynamics.

While dealing with feelings in prison is important. It may be easier to reach back in time to own yesterdays feelings under the guise of helping one's pre-prison community. In the Prisoner Professors book, there were many suggestions of topics that knowledgeable Prisoner Professors could write about to help other prisoners, staff and the families of everybody.

Of course, mental health is a professional specialty and none of us should be trying to manipulate people without the guidance of appropriate professionals. We can, however, fill libraries with guide books that may help prisoners in their independent reading when their feelings have been peeked in discussion groups.

It would be advantageous for Wardens to embrace appropriate resources that could be properly available and not break the institutional budget. Channeling feelings proactively can provide reasonable support for those who are troubled and also bring valuable balance to the whole community.

There is a depth of understanding needed about individuality that is not easily found in large meetings.

Efficiency is not just about containing prisoners for periods of time as ordered by courts of law in distant cities. Efficiency relates to the costs of the total system in a longer societal view as it impacts the here and now but also the future reactive consequences..

I have introduce this shift about money here because there is great importance to individuals and their feelings and their rehabilitation possibilities. Institutional delivery of understanding can seem very dictatorial and stifle possibilities for human integration that might allow healing for the long term and forever with no need to every come back.

Recidivism is a killer of community vitality that could be mitigated by reasonably expansive prison staff outreach.
If you wanted to be a farmer of positive community benefits, planting positive seeds early and often could reach a bountiful harvest for future citizens of your community.

10 - Correction Enforcement OR Coaching

In my book Prison Possibilities Correction Coaching Chapter 1, I wrote –

"Correctional Officers primarily keep people in jail and in control. Corrections Coaching could be an upward progression for correctional officers to grow their skill and their service to prisoners, facilities and the community.

The upgrade to coach status would include a utility for the prisoners, facilities and the communities that is new and multi-dimensional. The new role would include the use of skill to help the prisoners, facilities and the community by embracing a peaceful sentence serving and/or a realistic path to rehabilitation and release if they both work to make it possible.

This may not be right for every community and there may be some resistance to the concept. That position is part of the process of re-evaluation which is needed to improve prospects for living inside and/or rehabilitation and/or release.

There is not a clear path to the rehabilitation that I am proposing but the only thing that is abundantly clear is that we are not now being successful enough in that area.

Correctional officers are more familiar with most prisoners than any other contact within the system. That familiarity with sufficient time and opportunity can be a great asset in understanding the motivations of prisoners and discovering all the partnering potential for cooperative effort and benefit."

As I wrote that book, I became more and more vested in the possibilities for corrections officers to help create a new path out of the traditions that have existed for a long time. But that cannot happed without leadership and leadership can be a risky business.

I cannot imagine a day that stress is not a prominant factor for both correction officers and wardens. Stress can be a killer of many things for many people.

Many people who feel they cope with stress well can avoid the realities and process things in ways that seem to satisfy the pressures of every day. I have been concerned about stress for a long time and have a whole website dedicated to free information about dealing with stress.

The website is called http://www.StressReleaseCoach.com and it is free all the time and I encourage everybody to dig deep and often into the content. If you drain the swamp, the alligators can still get you.

I hope that your alligators can be contained and equal partner teams of your coaches and your prisoners can rise up and take charge of all risks for everybody that lives, works or visits within your walls.

It may be a Chinese proverb or anonymous but one quote that has helped me is "It is better to light one candle than curse the darkness."

The quote is a real stress buster that I was grateful to read and embrace. I sincerely hope you find it helpful also.

11 - Mental Health

Mental Health is very likely a no win topic for you. The Cycle seems perpetual.

There are many people who need to be cared for and there could be full mental health facilities on every corner if there were resources to reimburse providers. The resources seem to be lacking because government spending is out of control.

Spending by the governmemt seems lacking in many other areas. Do you remember when you were able to Satisfy the recommendations of those who you employ?

Tough times continue but I remain hopeful because I am outside the system and observing as much as I can. I also write as much as I can about possibilities and I remain hopeful that when we hit the point of considering options that are now not able to be considered, that there will be some value found in the ideas that I have documented.

I am hopeful that my prison possibilities invitations will get responses that can bear fruit in ways that I could never conceive. In my Prison Genius Pool Book, I ask –

"Some sources report that in America alone there are 2.3 million people or more in jail. How much do that many people know?
      The Answer is a whole lot."

I remain hopeful and I pray that a vein of Golden Answers can be found. Thank You God AND SO IT IS!

12 - Addiction

Another difficult topic for you is likely addiction. I have found that difficult also and that is what brought me back to the messages of Angel Raphael that started in 2013 and the messages about prisons that I channeled.

In the Introduction of *Angel Raphael Speaks Volume Four: Angels, Addicts, Alcoholics, and Prisoners – On Yeah!*, I wrote-

"Recently I was brought to Addiction as a focus of my writing as I see so much of it during Pastoral Rounds at the Hospital.

I just completed a book called *Angels Are Always Around Addicts and Alcoholics* and I did not realize that the completion coincided with a news media production called *Generation Addicted.*

The problem is enormous but the answers are few.

This morning the Angels are talking again to me a lot and I received new insight about turning lemons to lemonade.

While everything is still fresh I will work at integrating the vision, the previous messages and some new perspectives that need definition before words begin to make sense and be conceptual.

This book is about documenting all that along with a fresh integration with what came before."

In Volume 4, I integrated it all and laid out a realistic blueprint for a system changing set of ideas. The pages even included the fourteen messages from the Original *Angel Raphael Speaks – Prisons* E-Book (2013) and the eight additional Prison messages that came later.

Here is the full Table of Contents with the Page References

Table of Contents

13 - Jobs

The writing that gave me the most peace was the one related to creating job skills for prisoners by taking care of addicts and alcoholics when they are medically released from hospitals and in need of not returning to the temptations of their neighborhoods.

The idea is simple, if they go home – temptation will appear and they will be lost again or maybe forever. By keeping them in a contained care community run by prisoners, the prisoners get skills that convert to jobs later and the patient gets time to build willpower as the chemical and psychological hold continues to disperse.

Jobs for ex-prisoners are such a huge determining factor in the ability to survive on the outside.

Job competition with non-prisoners is hugely stacked against the prisoner getting a chance so an in-prison REAL training experience could make a huge difference.

Adding a couple of certifications like Patient Care Technician and Health Care Professional Cardio Pulmonary Resuscitation could further their appeal to a potential employer.

14 - Wrap Up From Volume 4

"Every Human struggles and gets lost in the frenzy of life so it is not at all unusual that society can develop also in an off target approach that seems to follow directly. Periodically evaluations can indicate that the target is being missed and reassessment is necessary. This is one such time.

The ideas expressed here are dramatically contrary to the normal security seeking patterns regulated by fear. There is a lot at stake here and the traditional patterns while logical are also unproductive and bankrupting us.

We are at a crossroads in the lives of the addicts and the alcoholics and the prisoners and we are also at a crossroads in the lives of the poor and starving children and also middle income families. Change is not only necessary but required. Absent Change, more misery is our destiny.

I do not know that the changes suggested here are an answer or just a warning flare but the Angels have been after me to translate the message in a way that good people can integrate it. I have tried and it is not an easy thing to do but now I transfer responsibility to those reading as you also are in this quagmire.

Do you want to change? The question is futile because we all know the answer is – NO. The obvious next questions is will you change? The Answer is not so certain!

I sincerely hope that you see the sincerity of this document and I hope this writing has not been futile. Whatever you do is ok for I have followed the directions and fulfilled my assignment.

We will have many days ahead and you get to determine how well they will be. Your power is more significant than you probably realize.

Even if your thoughts this minute are full of fear, you have power. A power frequently underappreciated is prayer because even if it changes nothing else, it changes you.

I have to think back to history again and reflect on some significant events. In 1492, Columbus set out on an adventure that forecast his vessel falling off the end of the earth. The end of the story worked out differently and well for many.

Once upon a time. England had a great problem with prisoners like we do now. England banished them to a foreign land where these unwanted people created a great land of their own and now the Queen visits them.

We can have fifty versions of new constricted environments that will maximize freedom, control risks, optimize and reorganize lives. Let freedom ring again with enough control.

The war is only lost if we surrender by giving up our power to fear. I encourage all readers to open their minds to the field of potential that flows from avoiding fear and following your bliss as you help everybody else do the same. Blessed be all of us."

15 - An Addiction Success Story

{From -Trauma Healing Options for VA Hospitals: Help for Veterans to Own Their Healing and Their Future}

The Man Shaking From Head to Toe

I went to do a pastoral visit on this day and as I entered the room, I saw a man who was shaking from head to toe. I introduced myself and asked if there was something that he wanted to Pray About (Pause), Talk About (Pause) or Complain about.

He laughed a shallow laugh but it was enough. He told me a story of disconnection from God because of his human experience with the church and why he could not go back. I explained to him that Philadelphia was a big city and if he didn't like that priest, he could go to another church or denomination until he found one suitable.

Making no headway, I told him about an exercise that I share called the Hand Up Handout. We did the exercise and he stopped shaking.

After lunch, I was walking past the room and I noticed that his hand was up in the air and I went in to check. I reminded him that once he reconnected with God, he could put his hand down. His reply was NOT YET!

Here is the Hand Up Handout

When things seem bad, it is very natural to feel down in the dumps and isolated and cutoff. There is both a physical and psychological dynamic to this isolation and the trauma that it supports.

23

I have found that the simple act of reaching the left, or receiving hand, up to God during prayer seems to make an awesome difference in the experience of all people and especially those who are depressed. The action taken seems to break them free of patterns of limited thinking and enables them to reconnect to the God who loves them so much.

Prayer by itself to many seems hollow because there is an expectation that nothing will happen but when they reach out and up there is a shift, an expectancy that things will be different. That expectancy breaks through some sort of mental disconnect obstruction mechanism and allows the mental obstacles to dissipate.

I find the Hand Up most effective when used with a customized prayer. The connection occurs within a second and the hand can be relaxed.

I invite you to reach out for breakthroughs in your life by connecting with the strongest power that there is – your creator.

I invite you to share this with those that need to be lifted up. Your caring and this technique may make the first shift that they have had in a long time .

May all who read this be blessed, AND SO IT IS.

Follow-Up Story

About twenty months later, I was paged at lunch. I answered and was asked to see a particular patient in a particular room.

The nurse told me that the patient was being discharged but refused to leave until he talked to me. I said Ok, I'll be right up.

I went in to the room and there was the man from the shaking story. He explained that since we last met he had been able to be free of his former addiction.

But he had just relapsed and within two days was re-admitted to the hospital. He saw me earlier in the hall and wanted an additional boost to help him be ready to go home.

*

Blessed Be All
Who Live, Work and Visit Prisons

Reverend Mike Wanner

For
Considering
These
Ideas

Ever

It Does Not Help Prayer Still Does!

Resource Site http://www.Create-A-Prayer.com

18 - Resource Books

Distant Healing Sessions (or Join Mail List) – Write To mikewann@voicenet.com

Books by Rev. Mike at www.Amazon.com

Veterans Healing Six Pack
1. *Trauma Healing Options for VA Hospitals: Help for Veterans to Own Their Healing and their future.*
2. *Trauma Healing Action Steps for Veterans: Help to Start Healing*
3. *Trauma Healing Action Steps for Veterans: Empowerment*
4. *Trauma Healing Action Steps for Veterans: Forgiveness*
5. *Trauma Healing Action Steps for Veterans: Thought Freedom*
6. *Tea For Veterans: Welcome One Home*

PTSD Power Pack:
1. *The PTSD Project: Turn Pain To Power*
2. *PTSD & Soul Retrieval: Putting One Back Together*
3. *PTSD & The Purple PAD: Calling all Scientists and PTSD Patients*

Angel Raphael Speaks Volume 1: Take Courage! God Has Healing in Store for You!
Angel Raphael Speaks Volume 2: Take Courage! God Has Healing in Store for You!
Angel Raphael Speaks Volume 3: Take Courage! God Has Healing in Store for You!
Angel Raphael Speaks Volume 4: Angels, Addicts, Alcoholics & Prisoners – Oh Yeah!
Angel Raphael Speaks Volume 5: Prisoners Caring for Alcoholics - Australia In Miniature Projects Intro
Angel Raphael Speaks Volume 6: Prisoners Caring for Addicts - Australia In Miniature For Addicts
Reiki Journaling from Japan
Reiki Is Alive: God's Great Gift
Four Parts to Healing
Distant Healing: We Are All Connected
Stress Release Energy Work: How To Cope
Does Reiki Love Heal Cancer?
Group Consciousness
Salute To Philadelphia VA Medical Center: Thank You
Reiki Transcript for Reiki 2 & 3 Channels: Dr. Usui Is That You?
God Bless Kindle & Amazon
Puppies Are Different From People
If Your Dog Dies
Toy Guns Are Obsolete
Great Spirit Made Children With Red Skin: AND

The Cage of Fear: Is Not Locked
God Made Children Red, Yellow, Brown, Black & White: Greet Each Child With
Kindness
Emergency Medical Kindness In The Cradle Of Liberty: Big City - Cracked Bell
Angels Are Always Around Addicts and Addicts: Help Is Near Now! Invite It In!
Angels Are Always Around Addicts and Alcoholics: Volume 2 - Tools To Help Re-Light
Your Life
Prison Jobs Now: Providing Care For Addicts And Addicts
Controlled Care Communities Concept
Prison Possibilities Dialogue Series: Concept
Prison Possibilities Dialogue Series: Volume 2, 3, 4, 5 Dialogues
Prison Possibilities Voluntary Exile
Prison Possibilities Corrections Coaches
Prison Possibilities For Mexicans: Is A Boat Better Than A Wall?
Prison Possibilities Family Time: A Reason to Thrive!
Prison Genius Pool: "So Much Genius In Jail"
Prison Possibilities Access Control: Prisoner Access by Request
Prisoner's Lawyers Can Save The American Economy: Make A Buck Doing It & Be
Thanked!
Prisoner Family Talks, Days, Stays & Vacations: Connecting Helps Healing
Prisoner Writing Projects: Write To Heal, Start Over & Reconnect
Prison Cell Clearing & Blessing: Clear Entities, Chase Ghosts, and & Create Sacred
Space
Prison Reiki? Maybe Someday? A Gateway To Help Heal Prisons & America?

Little Books at Kindle.com by Rev. Mike:
English Medical History Questionnaire For Non-English Speakers
English Language Helper For Non-English Speakers
Wise Wonderful Women Are The Well Of The Family
Answers for Test & Research: Dowsing Power
Crisis? Reiki! Baby? Reiki!
Bible References For Healing
Angel Raphael Speaks – Prisons
Angel Raphael Speaks – Veterans
The Saint Off Interstate 95

Angel Raphael Speaks through Rev. Mike Wanner. Please visit
http://www.AngelRaphaelSpeaks.com

19 - Angels Please Prayers

Addict's

Angels of Healing Selected
Help Me to Stay Directed
Come To Me From The Sky
I Am Ready to Succeed Not Try
If I Don't Invite You In
I Might Not Win
I Have Been Lost For Too Long
Help Me To Stay Strong

Alcoholic's

Angels of Healing On High
Help Me to Stay Dry
Come To Me From The Sky
I Am Ready to Succeed Not Try
If I Don't Invite You In
I Might Not Win
I Have Been Lost For Too Long
Help Me To Stay Strong

From

http://AngelRaphaelSpeaks.com/AAAAAAA/

20 - Private Channeling

Angel Raphael Speaks is a series of free messages that are channeled through Reverend Mike Wanner for the Highest good and Highest Healing of all concerned.

Many questions arise about Reverend Mike doing private channeling and he does help with that so e-mail him.

Reverend Mike is available world-wide as a psychic channel, emotional release facilitator, spiritual energy practitioner & teacher, and public speaker. He looks forward to meeting you soon!

Email - mikewann@voicenet.com 215-342-1270 PRIVATE SPIRITUAL READINGS/channelings or Spiritual Healing Sessions: Telephone or in person. Rev. Mike is available for private, one-on-one intuitive sessions with you, his Guide Family, and your Guides. He helps by offering clarity on emotional situations about your life, your purpose, your spirituality, and the release of stuffed emotions and cellular memory.

Connect to the love of your Guides today!

Contact Rev. Mike for an appointment.

Sessions available:

Spiritual Readings
Angel Channeling
Distant Reiki Healing
Distant Clearing of Stuffed Emotions
Distant Clearing Cellular Memory
Distant Clearing Energy Blockages
Distant Clearing of the Chakras
Customized needs
Mastermind dowsing responses to yes/no direction finding questions.

Rev. Mike is a facilitator of healing. He brings you and the Divine together so that you can align with the Divine and have a great time and a great life. All healing is between you and God, as it should be. Go ahead and start without Rev. Mike. Visit his prayer site http://www.Create-A-Prayer.com. Take the first step NOW.

21 - Reverend Mike Wanner

Rev. Mike Wanner started his metaphysical and ministerial studies with Reiki in 1993 and has studied seven styles of Reiki in the U.S., Japan, Canada, Denmark and Australia. He is certified to teach. He became certified to teach Integrated Energy Therapy in 1999 and co-taught the first IET class of the new Millennium. Mike began dowsing in 2001.

Ordained as a Metaphysical Minister of the International Metaphysical Ministry and an Interfaith Minister of the Circle of Miracles Ministry, Rev. Mike practices and teaches spiritual energy therapies in the Philadelphia Area.

Rev. Mike holds ministerial degrees from the University of Metaphysics and the University of Sedona. He is a Pastoral Care Associate of Aria - Frankford Hospital. He taught at the National Academy of Massage Therapy and Health Sciences.

Rev. Mike was a faculty member of the Medical Mission Sister's Center for Human Integration's School of Integrated Body/Mind Therapies in Fox Chase, Philadelphia, PA for twelve years.

Rev. Mike is licensed by the teaching of Intuitional Metaphysics to practice Spiritual Healing and Scientific Prayer. Mike is also a Prayer therapist.

Rev. Mike was elected in 2007 to the status of "Fellow of the American Institute of Stress."

In 2008, Rev. Mike became a practitioner of Coincidental Recognition as he incorporated the CoRe System in to his spiritual healing practice.

In 2009, Rev. Mike trademarked a new healing process called Quantum Quatro! Subtle Energy System Support®.

In 2011, Rev. Mike joined the outreach program known as the Health Advantage Group.

In 2012, Rev. Mike became a Certified Professional Coach by The Master Coaching Academy and Joined the Personal Empowerment Group.

Prior to his metaphysical, ministerial and coaching studies, Rev. Mike worked for Sears Roebuck and Co. while in High School and after graduation until he joined the U. S. Air Force in 1965. He returned to Sears from Vietnam in 1969 and stayed until 1978. His final Sears assignment was as an efficiency expert in Methods - Operational Research and Development.

He volunteered with Burholme Emergency Medical Services from 1969 and is still a Life Member and Board of Directors Member. He started a private ambulance company in 1975 and worked professionally in the field until 2001 when he devoted his full attention to real estate investing, healing, coaching and writing.

www.ReverendMikeWanner.com

www.ingramcontent.com/pod-product-compliance
Lightning Source LLC
Chambersburg PA
CBHW051419170526
45165CB00004BA/1885